~ PREFACE ~

What happens when poetry enfolds,
no trivial or relenting grasp, No
tender touch or half measure
it is here, the present, NOW!
Staking claim to deeper feelings
Not assigned to more suitable moments,
when convenience triumphs over urgency.
Often we are grabbed by the heart,
soul, the bollocks testing our strength
or weakness. And when in full
poetic flow release those inner emotions
that would otherwise vanish undisclosed
– LOST FOREVER.

Suggested recipe for the enjoyment of this book:

1. Distance yourself from all distractions.

2. Pour a good measure of your favourite tipple
   (minimum) at least 2 double measures.

3. Allow one hour of uninterrupted indulgence.

PS Don't lend the book to family or friends –
make them buy one.

Published in 2005 by Bob Lock
1 Gleneagles Court, Mafeking Road, Chatham, Kent
ISBN 0-9539693-1-2

Copyright © Bob Lock 2005

Bob Lock has asserted his right under the
Copyright Designs and Patents Act 1988
to be identified as the author of this work.

Typeset, printed and bound
by Multiplex Medway Ltd

~ CONTENTS ~

~

BROKEN
HEARTS

~

~ BEHIND THE CURTAIN ~

You sought little asking in return
even less, awaiting your first contribution
to womanhood. Fate, fortune's harbinger
of destiny chose the meeting chemistry
setting stage leaving us but players. No
in-depth rehearsals, tenderness forming
those early encounters pre-empting the outcome
spotlight dimmed, awaiting.

Warm summer sands bid welcome, the
picnic lunch you prepared with such
thought and care. Basking in warmth
of Sun, music from 'Porgy & Bess'. Then
the awaited liquid giving of glass and fluids
sating both thirst and bodies. But my
commitments taint the loving cup gone
its cheer, left only its inebriation to fuel
moments of passion or despair.

Your first love has survived but passing
years slowly erode, with time that last
goodbye (unaware when spoken) will provide
all that remains – memories.

~ OCEANS APART ~

Figment of dreams fulfilment of mine
you stand, move, lay, beautiful in
a land where dreams provide life's hope,
reality life's despair. Who formed
such beauty some unchallenged
invader within the depths of that
mighty Amazon? Whilst my Portuguese
flounders your 'Pigeon-English'
enchants, satisfying our daily needs.
But to you peers I remain an intruder
plundering their jungle rose.

Soon the inevitable leaving must
take place a final touch or tear,
the passing through airport security.
Touch of fingers prevented by panelled
glass, feeling the loss of warmth and
closeness, hearts heavy in parting's sorrow.
Now high up in the morning sky I
take my leave, below the mighty Amazon
in its own time threads majestically
through the endless green expanse.
Concealed within its magnificence
those predatory mysteries.

For hearts beat there too
(human and animal), fashioned
as in each of us driven by
survival, love, lust.
Pumping – beating – aching – breaking.
Living – loving – hating – dying.
Nothing changes life's cycle, that
dreaded predator time creates, the
providing and destroying both the beautiful
and the ugly at its own choosing.
Gifting itself to those who will survive
hearts joyful or broken.

~ YOUR BUS ~

After the passing of
years still to watch
that bus arrive where
only memories alight,
see you walk to
the door hear your footsteps
on the path.
Different this place
strangers passing by
as they have always done
now reflect your shadow.
To see that bus
watch you walk away
life's disillusion
heart's despair.
Regretted those three
unspoken words
five vowels, three consonants.

~ Coming of Age ~

It was not her beauty
Caught my eye and my breath
But her radiance, softly hidden
Like the Sun with dusk closing,
The piquant purity that
Brimmed naïve, impinging on
Heart and Soul.

I have often trod paths of liaison
Plumbed the depths of deceit
Tendering the rose of many thorns.
But this was different, somehow
Likened to love, the word abused
By philanderers and charlatans
Use in abuse.

Forget the firm flesh, carnal delights,
Exploitation, for those
Young arms bore welcome.
Paradoxically age and youth
Blending, self-reproach melting
Like snow in the new warmth
of a summer sun.

~ SORRY ~

You seek me out, I
await your presence
your voice floats in
the mind's shadow,
like the ebb and flow
of a mighty sea, filling
all corners with uncertainty.
Reverberating, my very sanity
brought into question.
Reminiscences flit
craving your acceptance.
Forgiveness would carry
its share of solace,
remorse its pain
contemplation its regret.

~ TOUCHING UTOPIA ~

Fingers reach out
Nerve ends caressed by expectation.
The mind, like a harpist searches for a note.
Awaiting, sweet the chord
Not only struck when music flows.

A touch, those fingers expressive and tender,
Pale sensuous, pink tipped promises of ecstasy.
Now to dream and wish,
For more than just digital fusion,
Progression to pleasures untapped.
No vocal discourse, eyes meet
Then return to pressing palms,
Each gentle touch speaking a thousand words.

If music be the food of love stay the symphony,
Till the score has been savoured.
Ingested, digested, to feed the need of fulfilment.
Not a singular selfish experience
But a shared and beautiful liaison
Of body and soul.

Blood flows under sensitive skin fusing.
A longing for more.
Each movement and touch teasingly
Telegraphs a message of inner desire,
What lies beneath? Words would intrude
On this interlude of touch and feel.
Fingers winging a message of intent,
"Open those gates", that I may enter
The inner sanctum.

~ True Love ~

*(In memory and dedicated to the
poetic style and rhyme of William Blake)*

If I fell from a tree,
Would my fall be broke by thee?

Or should I fall from off a cloud,
Would thou weep and wear a shroud?

And as I fell from out the sky,
Would the heart within thee die?

From these things – do I see
'Tis not me who dies, but thee.

~ HER FIRST LOVE ~

We walked with arms linked
Not long gone our childhood days.
Puberty's challenge overcome.
Sharing together those growing pains
Destined to live our lives as one,
Future's barometer set fair
But gone the summer now the snow
He says it's time for me to go.

My true love now has gone away.
In my mind, not only those handsome looks,
My eyes are but a camera,
My soul the photographer.
Now falling tears cloud the lens,
Then clear to reveal life anew.
Only the memories now, it seems,
That cling like ivy to my house of dreams.

~
REFLECTIONS
~

~ Untitled (1949) ~

There will come a time
When beauty's gone in this world of ours;
A time when men run everything
With great atomic powers,
When jets and rockets cross the sky
In precision and so-called grace
And everything that's natural
Has left the human race.

Think of our ancestors,
The days of serfs and slaves,
When human beings lived
In caverns and caves,
How times have changed since then,
For better or for worse,
For then was such a thing as peace
In this great universe.

~ NIGHT-TIME ~

Night-time is here the thought – divine
No toast to give, no special day.
Evening sun sinks below the line
Slowly, with every fleeting ray,
Heralding the close of another day.
Thoughts dart through the mind – like fireflies,
Alert – yet calm, to soothe, excite
Intruding on the fall of night.

Night-time is here, now begins
A casting out of daily sins,
Cast like thrown stones
It's all behind when night begins.
A gentle breeze fans the face,
No sound to intrude or mar the bliss,
This is such a special place
Made sweeter by a nocturnal kiss.

Night-time is here night brings
Special thoughts of many things,
Some warm, some happy or undefined
And some the day has left behind.
Can it continue? – Much to implore!
Let it last for evermore.
When night fades what more to say?
Lord, help guide me through another day.

~ Our Choice ~

As we watch the old year die
Etched in pyrotechnic sky,
Will the fires of delight
Live for more than just one night?

Now the new Millennium's here
Forged our hopes, like a mighty spear.
Its shaft wrought in furnace fires
And cast on wings of our desires.

Are forged the shackles of our heart,
Long before the fires start?
As we hear pundits weave their word
That so often perish at the sword.

To predict the future – and our fate
Two thousand years humanity waits.
For one last hope, our plight to stem,
A reincarnate from Bethlehem.

~ CHILDHOOD IN THE EARLY 1940s – 'AUNTY ROSE' ~

I remember those childhood days. Sleeping under the kitchen table as in deep dark of night marauding Luftwaffe wreaked its toll of destruction, raining down a multitude of explosives with grim determination. Following days however were mostly normal and life continued except for the unfortunate casualties.

One such day, the summer sun burnt highways and paths deep and incessant melting their tarmac overcoats. Tyres warming from the heat, clear sky heaping further onslaught. Its blueness heralding the visitor whose arrival would explode the day's calm with untold ferocity. Aunty Rose a human flurry of perspiring animation, bounding through the door like a guided missile, set to explode on impact with any unsuspecting humanity.

"Young Bert!" her voice echoing from all four walls with mega amplification. "Young Bert! I am here, where are you lad? There you are – not hiding I hope? Let aunty see your knees – clean I trust and your hands, no reward for grubby boys." I cringe, mutter silently, words not meant for the ears of doting aunts (or Sunday School Teachers). "What's that lad? Speak up! Brought you something nice." I fidget thoughts turning to bent wire and wondering whether her knicker elastic would successfully propel stones from my catapult. Not then knowing that I would have needed something much stronger.

"I've brought you this poppet." My eyes scanned the carrier bag with mixed expectancy and apprehension. "You'll like this" she boomed multi-ringed fingers delving deep for the promised treat. Then, she proudly displayed the contents, wrapped in tissue paper – a golden sovereign and a photograph of Grandad*. "Asked me to bring it" she said, "he isn't well enough to visit you himself, ill in bed – the doctor's not happy."

I clasped my gifts thinking of Grandad's last visit. How we sat in the garden, his stories and how he would be continually lighting his pipe – sometimes letting me strike the matches. Then making smoke come from his ears. Reciting the tune 'Run Rabbit Run' and saying how his favourite song was 'Underneath the Arches'.

Grandad died soon after, but mum said he had gone to heaven and that it was too far away for visits. I remember laying in bed thinking – I must ask mum in the morning "Will God allow Grandad to stay in heaven? Lighting all those matches – after all there is a war on."

*Referral to Grandad at that time was in fact Great Grandfather Albert Edward Barrett.

~ A Garland of Poppies ~

Wrong place wrong time.
Right place right time.
Each definition (right or wrong)
rides the clock face, as
its hands despatch moments
of hope or despair.
Cog tick, heart beat.
Cog tick, heart beat.
Hands move, metallic fingers
holding their grasp on eternity.
Flanders fields, wrong place
for brave men, right place
for scavenging rats.
Now, gone the animosity
atrocity tempered in remembrance
by poppies, petals shed –
Blood red.

~ GRANDAD ~

(A tribute to Frederick George James)

You look out from
an old photograph
black on grey, a
tinge of sepia framing
the passing of years.
Your smile radiates
from the heart,
Kindness matched only by
care and understanding.
Mentor to my childhood
comfort in war's darkness.
Now having all but
matched your living age
I live in your shadow,
self reproach and remorse
weigh heavy on conscience
like an invading army.
May your example
wasted in life, bring
comfort in death.

~ You Shouldn't Have Told Me Mum ~

I am the onion man
Who cried at the bank,
I am the Sinatra
Who could never be Frank,
I am the tripod
That walks with a limp,
I am the child
Spawned by a wimp.

I am the mentor
Of sorrow and pain,
I am the alien
Who made it to Spain,
I am the singer
Who can't sing a note,
I am the victim
Knife at his throat.

I am the egg
That fell from the wall,
I am the dwarf
Who never stood tall,
I am the loner
Who feels the pain,
I am the sunbather
Caught by the rain.

I am the offspring
Held by the mouse,
I am the black sheep
At Somerset House,
I am the error
Trapped here on earth,
I am the bastard
An outcast at birth.

I am.

~ The Silent Cot ~

You wear your silence, your
moth breath flickers like
a slow candle, painfully inaudible
even at still of night.

Our newborn daughter, heaven's
blessing challenging all known
perfection. Fear prevents all
thought of sleep.

I listen for a movement, cry
or whimper, cross the room
gently press an ear to your tiny face,
silhouetted in half light.

No sound, apprehension, my
questioning finger prods seeking
slightest movement, assurance that
all is well, uneasy I return to my bed.

In half slumber I am awakened
at early dawn by your cry, like
the soft wail of a siren. Move to
hold close your tearful trembling body.

And thank God, thank God.
Hating that silence the uncertainty.

~ Empty Hooks ~

A cold merciless wind, cuts
Its swathe across the slow tide
Creeping ever shoreward. A twice
Daily ritual of silent approach.
Yard by yard, slowly swamping
Near endless acres of foot
Squelching mud and occasional
Quicksand.

Gone the carefully laid dead line,
Fishermen's ploy of patient noncommittal.
Fish no longer plentiful, their ever
Diminishing number – culling's stern
Legacy. I tread the beach – recall past years,
Rewarding catches of dab, flounder, plaice,
The occasional large skate, hear my
Children's shrieks of delight – their awe at
each gift from Neptune's vaults.

Four decades pass almost unnoticed,
Like the fish now seldom seen on the
Chill winter sands of Weston-Super-Mare.

~ HOMELAND ~

(A tribute in memory of R.S. Thomas)

I open your book run my fingers
over cold paper – words
(like braille) rise clear from the pages.

Master manipulator of adjective
Glorious, oh so glorious artistry, words
reaching to heart and soul.

I visit your Welsh homeland, borne
on the wings of each stanza. Noisy
tractor, plough tilling the brute earth

a lone figure docking mangolds with
futility's cold blade, portraits of your
ancestry cascading in sentences, stanzas.

Felt your resentment, desperation.
"Rest now your hand", may God fashion
a new land of your dreams.

~ SEARCHING ~

Night nurtures dark cloaked effigies,
In sombre stance, mid ancient trees.
Viewing their wizened warps
With deep held breath,
Awaiting a requiem chant to death.

Flap winged bats in silent flight
Radar in on shafts of light,
As moonbeams dart from darkened clouds
In stern defiance of night-time's shroud.

The yew that so long has stood,
A cynical interweave of wood.
With roots sunk deep in hallowed ground
Seeking answers – yet unfound.

Buried lies the related oak
Encasing souls, perhaps in flight
Searching mysteries of the night.
Musty mould, the tombs surround
Awaits their return and answer found.

~ MOMENTS IN TIME ~

Allow me to introduce myself – I am
'Moments', those brief occasions known as
transitory influences. You may sometimes find
our relationship special even magical when
allowed to be objective (or adjective). We can
share truth, joy, other emotions though my
presence sometimes fleeting.

Then there is my sibling 'Time'
the more lasting influence who on occasions
may appear idle, remain motionless,
but generally active sharing daily pleasantries.
Feel free to choose him or wait for me whichever
you prefer, we both are available.

Watching over us our paternal influence
'Father Time' builder of long term relationships
well versed in destiny, waiting to make
your acquaintance. We each have limitations,
difficulties, but enjoy involvement in daily life,
distancing ourselves from 'clichés'.

'Time' (the more infinite and continued
progress of existence) and I, often work
in close accord each apportioning.
Sometimes he is guilty of gathering my
attributes (accumulating moments) though
numerically we both stand up to be counted.
I gather you wish to consolidate our relationship.
"Not a moment too soon!"

~ TWICE THE LOSER ~

The pen strikes, with
Cobra-like determination its
Red venom spreading life's
Blood thin. The settler's
Delight – His daily contribution
To the conglomerate.
Juggling betting slips. Death's
Disciple to the gambler's dream.
Pain etched faces mirror
Years of frustration, credibility
At one with disillusion.
Lady luck – Virginal, stands
Contemplating her followers, witnessing
Them fucked with no resort to
Sexual fulfilment. Their marital
Relationships often wasted like
The years of indulgence. Wages
Spent, like love's lost promise.

~ THE FOX ~

Full moon throws light spears
parting laden clouds, the chill wind
scatters powdered snow, spreading
like icy talc – holding my skin in cold caress.
A Fox appears, sleek, silent,
stealthy steps cushioned. A lone car
passes wheels skimming packed snow.
The Fox watches, stops for a moment
silhouetted, statuesque in moon glow.
An eerie silence returns, our every
movement accentuated by the white
stillness, sharing moments – alone
in our own worlds.

Now, long gone winter's hold the green
tide of spring blossoms into full summer.
I look out on a shaded green lawn.
Fox with vixen saunter tentatively from
tree's shadow, sees me framed by the
window but moves easily closer. They
roll on the soft grass, he stands, stretches,
tenderly nibbling his partner's ear. For
some time they romp lazily, then, with
just a glance casually move off, returning
peacefully to their woodland existence.
Once more, our worlds close only as nature
and civilisation allow.

~ LIFE GOES ON ~

Tiny tots in torn trousers
Meter Maids in laundered blouses,
Night shift workers deep in sleep
Indulgent shirkers deep in debt.

Clapped out motor on the street
Road tax due felt the threat,
Down the dole for a hand out
Chip-butty roll for a tuck in.

Dad's just died, comes the hearse
Last lone ride expect the worst,
Funeral bill through the door
Equity nil through the system.

Tiny tots in torn trousers
Meter Maids in laundered blouses.

~ AT THE WINDOW WITH IMOGEN ~

(Summer 2000)
(For my Granddaughter)

Distant street lights part
early morning mist, flickering
like candles in empty jars.
Through window-pane
a solitary sunbeam reflects
the soft blue of young eyes,
summer flora folding inward
seeking mutual admiration.
A lone bird dwells
in your fledgling eyes
your sweet breath distills the air,
soft cheek offering tender caress.
The touch of a symphony in diminuendo
diminishing all life's pain in one cadenza.
Stolen moments of which we all dream
each second ticking away
like a heavenly clock.

~ ORDINARY FOLK ~

It's hard to fathom – this world!
a funny old place, when you remember
to laugh. We are warned about the
perils of booze, promised a dire fate
when hitting the bottle but breweries
and off-licenses continue to prosper
no-one you know seems to die of
alcohol poisoning. Even when
dehydration kicks in and the world
spins a little faster with a five degree
tilt, followed by hours building bridges
over the dreadful void.
Some say 'life is for living' that's fine
whilst that hole in the wall keeps
disgorging its filthy lucre in a desperate
attempt to avoid a head-on clash
with the nearest J.C.B. And the car you
promised yourself for next Christmas arrives
on the first of April and the bit of skirt
across the street finishes first in the
'cleavage' stakes in frantic pursuit of
the early morning bus (something worth
getting out of bed for).

Then giving your name when paying
your paper bill, referral to a
customer delivery number, together with
the newsagent's scowl – like a camel
with an attitude problem.
Of course you remain just a number
(better though when less obscure)
Lucky Seven, less fortunate thirteen,
Key of the door twenty-one or maybe
a touch of sixty-nine wouldn't go amiss.
But of course number ONE would
be the ideal. It's nice to be somebody
when you're nobody.

~ GIVING IT UP ~

Having passed three score
years and ten, rid my mind
of equine, benefactors cancelled
'Racing Post' orders and dispatched all
instant credit facilities to the
wheelie-bin life hasn't changed much.
Race meetings come and go
withdrawal symptoms kick-in –
occasionally, the bank balance
continues on an upward curve.
New pursuits combat the tedium and
time un-spent piles up. Time to
contemplate – a less stressful daily
journey past the undertaker's parlour.

~ SAFE JOURNEY ~

They sit, neat tidy rows
Charing Cross – rush hour
another crowded commuter snakes
silently from a London station.
For some, each scheduled stop
bringing familiar surroundings,
cars, journey's end.
Loners, spouses, loved ones
now observed and monitored,
prey to the opportunist, abductor, mugger,
the extra cost of your ticket a
twenty-first century overhead.
The price paid is not predetermined
or negotiable but reliant on fate,
percentages defying the comfort of
security. One more sadness in a world
where unawareness and naïvety
often prove – the death of reason.

~ IN THE POST ~

Another day, morning dreams on hold
Clock face early, luminous,
Timeless in light silhouette of dawn.
A sudden rattle of door furniture
Pre-empts the now familiar thud of
Buff envelope – flotation or receivership?

Poetic challenge buoyant as blue chip.
Critical review, architect of
Castles in the air, words cutting
Deeper than a surgeons scalpel
To reach both heart and Soul.
Where hope blossoms or dies
Sentence by sentence.

Deep study of comment, Advice, Criticism.
The aspiring bard will not
Don his cloak today, but continue
The cost of his poetic license.
Human milk not always kind
But with dedication – will maybe,
Nurture and sustain tomorrow's success.

~ INSOMNIA ~

Silent I lay endless night
surrounds, awake seeking that
elusive dream. Restless, turning,
awaiting Morpheus' comforting cloak
but only sleeplessness prevails.
Thoughts of success, failure,
happiness or sorrow pre-empt
tomorrow's outcome. Another day
creeps nearer, an early sun warms,
a crescendo of light filling the
horizon with an eye-blinding glow,
Orange and red staking claim
to total supremacy. Dawn
heralds another day, time for hopes
unaccomplished, challenges unmet,
dreams unfulfilled.

~ Journeys Too Late ~

The sea carries,
All but those who
In dreams journey.
Nor' skies lift those who
Travel on imagination's wing.
Leaving only floating clouds
And fleeting shadows
On which to reflect.
The moon dusts
Far off shores,
Unvisited beaches
Other feet now tread.
Blurring the vision with sand
That trickles, like a timer
In the mind's eye.
Pebbled shores
Crave attendance
In stoney silence.
Awaiting once heavy feet,
That now so lightly tread
An impromptu stairway.
Its destination, of fate's
Design and choosing
As time runs out.

~ TOMORROWS ~

What shall tomorrow hold
will it make an appearance?
To arrive and depart
would be considered normal
to pause confusing
not to arrive inconceivable.
Tomorrows bring moments
in which to live,
our present our future
time in which to reflect.
Without them
emptiness washes over.
Its void imponderable
the darkness irreversible
outcome unthinkable.

~ STEPPING ON THE GAS ~

Shining chrome, red paint
In distance grows faint.
Rev-counter meeting its match
In a suicidal dash.
Feeling the maximum input
of little man – big foot.

~ ALZHEIMERS ~

Grey mist envelops, empties
the mind – thoughts drift outward,
No longer birds hammer home
their shrill notes.
Castles fall to echoes
darkness engulfs, soul
drawn screaming to the Moon.
Left only shattered fragments,
minds that built empires,
tore limbs in conflict, ate
the heart of civilisation.
Einstein's triumph, the fuehrer's
'Mein Kampf', Judas deception.
Leaving posterity to contemplate.

~ FLEDGLINGS ~

Across winter's stark terrain
Spreads the green tide. Spring buds
Burst their bonds of languidity
Sun shedding its winter overcoat.
Earth exhales in the season's
New-found glory.
A glory shared with new arrivals
Nature's Animation born on wings
Of wonder, facing now the mystery
And challenge of life.
Fledglings, young wings not yet
Mobilised, free fall from their
Nests in precarious descent like
Shuttlecocks or on invisible parachutes.
Stumbling dazed into their
New world.

~ Living ~

Earthly presence and its grasp
Governed by fate's mighty rasp.
Is placed together bit by bit,
Sometimes to find no pieces fit.
One day life's destiny
May wash upon us, like a sea.
And carried by its mighty tide
Stand us tall, the surf to ride.

So take the pleasures of each day,
Lest 'The Reaper' calls, respects to pay.
And to the trickle of time's sand,
Dance a sombre saraband.
Though coming days may be brief,
Drink well, from 'the cup of life'.
To quench the pain and sorrow
At the thought of no tomorrow.

~ TREES ~

In nature's rich tapestry the ace is played
On warm summer days provider of shade,
Branches like arms reach to the sky
Songbirds' delight on a bough set high.
For birds the end of daily flight
Peace and comfort – home for the night.
Each tree perceived the more enjoyed
Loss of which would leave such a void.

Silver Birch, Willow, Sycamore too
In gardens stand, of various hue.
Adding their magic, joy to behold
Joined by a Beech copper and gold.
The London plane tall and stark
Absorbing life's air devoid of its bark.
Mighty Oaks of stature and girth
Spreading roots deep in the earth.

Little surpasses the Ash and Oak
So many of these sadly bespoke,
'John loves Joan' in bark cut clear
Carved memento, shed of a tear.
Tilia vulgaris no act from a show
Botanically named, the Lime does grow.
The mighty Sequoia on distant land,
Like 'Custer' makes defiant stand.

Castania and Aecelus add to the fun
Sweet Chestnuts, Conkers, produced by the ton,
A schoolboy dream… 'Stringer six'
Battle with conkers in playground mix.
Autumn leaves shed – majestic and stark
Snow-covered status alone in the park,
Knowing nature will brighten their lives
In coming months when Spring arrives.

Trees in life, from seed and pod
Are surely a gift – direct from God.

~ THE MELTING POT ~

From our roots
Generations grow
Through the warm earth.
A pyramid of existence
Rising from the ashes
Of our ancestry.
Genes forge the links
Of Hereditory's chain,
Its tensile tested
As we form a tree
Of human life.
Now, gradually emerges
The new generation. A
Wondrous universal mosaic
Bursting all bonds of origin,
As skin tones portray
World wide integration
Of our ever merging,
Beautiful human race.

~ WORDS, LEAVES AND PAGES ~

Poetry you give so much but
eternally ask nothing in return
your contribution free to all.
Comfortable homes, smart cars,
indulgences bear their cost.
Your words cannot be bought
but at opportune moments fall
like leaves from a tree. Many admire
the foliage, disturb those leaves
tread their crispiness but few
find the words human endeavour
fails to dislodge. May those
who convey your message rejoice
in their privilege and as
leaves spread your words remain
for both page and posterity.

~ An Apology ~

*(To my friend (and Minister)
The Rev. Ralph Seelig*)*

You started the Box-car ride
'My Mentor'
wheels that would skim
S.E.8 and outward. Providing
Zephyr, Zodiac, transporting
my body, my spirit of adventure
'Negotiator of sales'.
Your hand fashioned my existence
hope and future, whilst
controlling your own mobility.
Javelinda, Squeezy, your even
three wheeled unpretentiousness.
On your back seat a second hat,
suaveness pandering to humility
in the despatch and production
areas of The Borough and Tooley Street
where clients often showed
their resentment of 'flash gits'.
Then there were forays into
Victoria Street – the inner sanctum
of W.1. Contractors to the building
industry. The sumptuous lunches,
visits to Lords, The Oval, Wimbledon.
An admiring peep at the nubile
exertions of a young Virginia Wade.

You fashioned my outer being, honed
its carcass to social acceptability,
releasing the inner spirit.
No mentor could have controlled
or tamed that inner beast, which
only now slowly dies from
remorseful bludgeoning. Its swathe
through life decimating the
forest timbers from which sprang
my future hope.

*Ralph Seelig was at the commencement
of early working days my Sales Manager.*

~ BEWARE!
THE DEVIL'S THERE ~

Lucifer his seed does sow
On hallowed ground, his chosen foe.
Testing the trident of his might
In disarming hell-fire's light and
Threatens those who turn blind eyes,
With purgatory eternal, upon demise.

Sends the sanguine spirit in full flight
A cavorting caprise at fall of night.
Or on gossamer wings, that can fool
The astute and most wary ghoul.
Whose spirit of nocturnal play
Lives at night, but dies by day.

And with doubt the mind infests
A soulful epitaph of bereft.
Casting his spell on all around
Incarcerate in captive ground.
Retains the body by hold of earth,
Absorbs the soul and shuns rebirth.

~ Moving Onward ~

Friendly pub – busy bar staff
Buzz around, jokes, innuendo.
'Same again Dave?' – Life
As we know it, tidy – conventional,
Undemanding at lunchtime leisure.
Canned music pounds a slot machine
Whirls, clanking meagre rewards
For those of infinite patience.
Hardly noticed, a frail figure
Accompanied yet so alone sits
Toying (Going through the motions)
With a glass of wine. Her actions
In accordance with those expected
But lethargically muted.
Outwardly alive, but the eyes
Convey a different conclusion – open
But dead, life, long since departed.
You look, understand, futility and
Resignation screaming out,
Other life must surely await.

~ DEATH LURKS ~

The brief clearing from jungle dense,
Offered a welcome, though momentary,
Opportunity of rest and relief.
Hat cast aside and over-worked machete
Thrown to earth for physical respite.
Fate awaits, its deadly message to deliver.
Silence – too silent, almost un-noticed a
Stealthy rustle of nearby foliage
Heralds a dangerous confrontation, a
Swaying, glistening disciple of impending doom.
He is closer than comfort decrees;
His thrown shadow all but cloaks
The swaying menace. The deadly venom coil
Vies with the shadow, threatens, but hangs still.

'King Cobra', the homage of its reptilian kingdom
Observed without question,
Conceived by hand mightier than man.
Meanwhile a nearby ant colony seeths.
Its strong back in merciless toil,
Their endeavour defying human comparison.
Silence reigns and nothing moves or
Nothing that would take eternity to task.
He knows any movement will
Encourage fierce fangs
From languidity into instant action.
The sun spews down its searing heat
From molten bowels;
Baked earth powders under slightest movement,
He seeks desperately escape.

Twigs snap pressured by tread, carrying
The extra burden of anguish heaped shoulders.
A flinch, a change of eye contact.
Little! But on this occasion – more than enough.
The cobra strikes – pain! Then
A raging kaleidoscope of life's memories
Flood through mind and brain.
Soon he is no more.
The victor's unchosen task complete,
He slithers cynically away, to face
The cruel and threatening world,
Of jungle's making.
The silence is broken, sound returns
As nature switches the volume to normality.
"Why?" we ask, do these things happen?
God only, knows.

~ DREAMS END ~

Once more a venture into the realms of
somnolent dream, visions and fantasy.
Daily life left behind,
Ahead a journey into surrealism.
What facade will present itself in slumber?
The heart beats, pounds,
Fighting to drive body and mind to seek reality
And discard fantasy – to no avail;
What is happening? 'I am skating'.
I skate with flowing ease.

Paths all around holding ice,
My feet holding ice – it holds me to earth
I skate, destination unknown.
Will journey's end be home or eternity?
I skate, float, never to question,
Not to ask for reason why.
I look for buses (life's routine) – there are none.
Fading reality coaxes the mind
Into wonderment and question,
What purpose this mystical journey?

The mind fights to sustain reality
But calls out in despair, pleading for respite,
Such dreams must have purpose.
After all! Nature gave us sleep paralysis
To protect, and deter bodies afloat.
Sometimes, I fly or fall
The experience – wondrous elation.
Then that seemingly endless plunge
To journey's-end, does oblivion beckon?
Semi-awakening as body returns to earth
Bed sheets offering shroud-like cover,
How strong is life's hold?

That flight from earth questioning sanity
No wings of alcohol's making
But sobriety called still to question.
I pull back to bed's womb like comfort
Security, peace, warmth.
Am I still here?
Will the next journey
Be to hell and back? Or
Will it be to Utopia?
Shall I, be invited?

~ COME THE ZOMBIES ~

Beware! human puppet, animation's toy
what hand controls your strings?
Gives birth to daily song and dance,
Chords on which life's music is played.
Vulnerable marionette cherish those moments
For they who live no melodies
Will seek control of bodies that flap
Like broken wings and manipulate
To dance in their delight.
For they are made of no music
Unborn in life's orchestration
And bear the silence of endless interlude
Awaiting the drum of a heart that will pound
As theirs.

~ A Time of Rest ~

Evening shadows lengthen,
Dusk paying homage to
Sun's capitulation.
Night moves swift,
Darkness advancing
Like a conquering army,
Marching feet stamping the
Demise of another day.
Morpheus, cloak now drawn,
His somnolent nocturne
Filling the soul with
Peace and Tranquillity,
Moments to dream.

~ THE SILENT PHONE ~

Why do you not ring?
Are we engaged in some
silent vendetta speak
sustain our relationship
reactivate those voices from the past.

Speak to me why are you silent
did I offend or hold you
too close you once spoke
long and sincere why are you
so detached call now I
still have strength to hold you.

Time was I could live
without you do you punish me
for my noncommittal,
arrogance, neglect, please ring
awaken that darkness dispel
the nothingness of silence.

Once you would ring often
bring the world alive tolerating
my misdemeanours, listening
(offering no advice) but always
aware patiently observing
relationships, errors.

Let us relive past journeys
conquests even abject moments
of pain, despair, failure. You
spoke to me then when I
found the desire to listen,
sometimes unaware of your presence.

Now you hold my future
your eternal life will see
new generations, new worlds
long after my demise. You remain
silent still do not ring. Is it
something that I have said?

~

SMILES

~

~ A Complete Service, Undertaken ~

The wife of John – a packaging boffin
Approached us to supply a light-weight coffin.
But before the time of his demise
Was unaware of the impending surprise.
Apparently John, of whom it was said
"Spent his last earthly moments in bed."
Was known to have died in excitements prime
Hence the reason for his 'incline',
Which made it hard for Terrence and Syd
Whose job it was to close the lid.
Syd then phoned us with a stutter and stammer,
So we sent in our team, with nails and a hammer
To close the lid and fulfil our promise
Of service 'extended' to each John
– And Thomas!

~ NATURISM (STARTING FROM SCRATCH) ~

Naked rambles
What a shambles!
Bodies ravaged by
Nettles and Brambles.
Sturdy trainers
Protect the feet
But above trouble lies
For tender calves
And inner thighs.
As Scots-thistles
And spiky twigs
Activate obnoxious jigs.

~ ENDOWMENT ~

This is the tale of my
Amorous cutlery and tableware.
It transpires much woo(ing)
To(ing) and Fro(ing) has been
Going on behind my back.
Plates taking a shine to dishes
Only to finish all washed up.
Knives and spoons in close
Embrace, finding their relationship
Severely shaken by forked tongues.
Drinking vessels cupping hands
Around each other, finding
Their grasp hard to handle.
Dinner plates enjoying snug loving
Contact finishing in tears.
Saucers their saucy antics
Dampened – Now in deep water.
Killing nursery rhyme stone dead,
The dish and the spoon
Have recently parted company,
Deciding to go their separate ways.
Now, they have all ran away
With the dishwasher
Who, it would appear
IS ANYBODY'S!

~ Miners Can Be Politicians ~

Upwardly mobile coalminer Kenny
Auctions his thoughts for a penny,
Once again abundant takers
From the host of 'left in wake'rs'.
Coins flipped by double your stake'rs,
Tell a tale.
After all it would be a dread
To be ahead, of the situation.

Kenny you see holds their fate
Entering now the political gate.
Left behind, his modest dreams
Etched upon the coalface seams.
No longer just the scuttling rats
To bedazzle with his torch light hats,
A new challenge metred out
By society and politicians.

Kenny with his new found power
Doffs flat cap in ivory tower.
Now a subject of daily inspection
By deft exponents of verb and interjection.
Horoscope future, outlined in the stars
Predict 'status symbol' jaguars.
His followers and ardent voters
In lesser motors – follow his progress.

Time the miners had some clout.
Amongst the 'hard baked' upper crust
Whose feet had never trod the dust,
That life's hard smitten – had so often bitten.
But now we have a sudden blip
Ballot boxes, that shoot from the hip.
Hence the reason for dejection,
Kenny's party has lost the election.

~ LEONARDO ~

I am a dab-hand with my brush
That is why I'm always flush,
Each evening to Barclays with my loot
In brogues and my Carnaby suit.
Then I join the taxi rank
Here comes my cab – a 'Sherman Tank'.

My favourite saying is 'Reach for the sky'
They call me *Gene Autrey – I wonder why?
I tell them it should be *Buck Jones
With my mastery of pastel tones.
My ambition is to paint a fridge
Or 'One Way' signs on Clifton Bridge.

As I climb my ladder to the stars
Strengthened by a lunch-time Mars,
I think one day for a spoof
I'll paint a chimney – or a roof.
I finished the 'Muriels' and garden gnome
So maybe next the Millennium Dome.

My customers seldom complain
And pay me double to work in the rain.
Now master of my occupation
I donate my services – to the nation,
And with my good pals 'Bill and Ben'
Will paint the ceilings at Number 10.

("See you Tony!")

Cowboys in the 1940s.

~ DON'T KNOCK IT ~

Flight of fancy, land of dreams
Benidorm bursting at all seams.
Flowing sangria caressing lips
Wild Paso Dobles, swaying hips.
Destination of the brave,
Indulgence, the peseta's slave.
Contemplation, will this pleasure end?
Next year it might be Southend
– Or Margate!

~ CREDENTIALS ~

Aspiring poet, seeker of the
laureateship you should know
a single word can determine
success or failure. Is this why
whilst the world vociferates you
remain silent awaiting that
opportune moment. You may be
thwarted by that dreadful predator
'writer's block' which, though a
hindrance will fail to deter.
With strength of mind you must
succeed. Never contemplate failure,
pen the ultimate, move forward,
surpass the icons, overtake those
who flounder in mediocrity. You
have the character – but your C.V.
is bollocks!

~ Names ~

Take heed! names engender
credence, credibility their forte.
Conversationally they can remain
unspoken, gently introduced or
on special occasions 'dropped'
at an appropriate or opportune
moment. Who can trust or
welcome the inference 'Mr Somebody'.
As descriptive nouns
names structure our understanding.
On a personal plain specifying
and identifying each individual.
Consider carefully the importance
of remembering names, fail
at your peril.
"Excuse me!
Haven't we met before?
Who did you say you were?"

~ Reflections ~

I travel the train,
Life's outcome reflected
In carriage windows,
'Fat ugly old man'.
Not a thin ugly old man
Or a fat handsome old man,
each reflection tells
Its sad story.
Who invented mirrors?
Allow me a few
Moments with him
In a dark alley.
It's most unfair! There
Should be modified
Old people's homes for
Fat ugly old men,
With provision for special
Needs (puns excused)
Where self-esteem and
Confidence are available
In lieu of Viagra, which
Is of course, little use to
'Fat ugly old men'.

~ RESPONSES – THICK OR WHAT! ~

A wingless bird with joy flutters
Power cut, the gas lamp stutters.
Buttresses – just been buttered
Doors ajar with windows shuttered.

'I say – Well well!'

Hastings conflict watched by cattle
Francis Drake in Seattle
Queen Victoria's pram had not rattle
Agincourt was Nelson's battle.

'Fancy that – History!'

Underground, seeking vistas
Gondolas in Seven Sisters
W. G. without his whiskers
Seven nuns dressed as misters.

'Oh! – Strange!'

Lavender scented stocks
Wreaths of purple Hollyhocks
Lotus blooms, grown in woks
Gardeners gloves – without a fox.

'My! My! – Horticulture!'

Fairies punching out the lights
Unicorns jousting with knights
'King Kong' tearing maidens tights
Hot dogs, with vicious bites.

'Oou – Violence!'

Saki with Angastura Bitters
Fresh chop-sui fritters
Bird's nest soup with the squitters
Geisha girls are baby sitters.

'Oriental – Hark at me!'

Strawberries, without their flecks
Cyclops in 'Dennis Taylor' specs'
Librarians with sound effects,
Nubian Tarzans with no pecs.

'Phonies!'

Golden ingots red with rust
Sahara bought by the National Trust
Noddy wracked with wanton lust
Steptoe joins the upper crust.

'Really? Well I never did!'

'Fisticuffs' means to have a fight
We can see only in the light
Day always follows night
Black is the reverse of white.

'Ridiculous – Don't be so silly!'

~ CANDLELIGHT ~

Candle how you burn so bright!
In the darkness of the night.
Held by form of callow youth
Not to feel your tallow move.
Aware not as that flame does melt
That from which your body's smelt.
In youth, a noble artefact;
In death, no more than molten wax.

Pray that we show no mirth
Who lit the flame to give you birth.
In your body no flesh or bone
Your heart sustained by wick alone.
Each burning moment in time,
Shortening that inner spine.
In your life, no acclaim
Or chance to grace those halls of fame.

As your outer light does flow
Gladdened by no inner glow,
Your Destiny and fate pre-planned
By the touch of human hand.
Never do you work abort
To make your earthly days less short.
Able not to shed a tear!
Knowing that life's end is near.

Disfigured cameo of fate
Oblivion knocking at your gate.
Gone those symbols of your might,
Now a waxen stalagmite!
That flame you burned with such desire
Sustained through life, whilst mortals tire.
In your last death – throws on earth
"Forgive Us Please!" Who gave you birth.

~ DEPARTURE ~

When I see no beauty
in jade or Ming,
no longer hear
church bells ring.
Each stone and arrow
has left its sling,
love has gone,
life 'a thing' and
my heart does
no longer sing.
Dear Lord, send
angels to carry me
on their wing.
To Heaven!

~ INDEX OF FIRST LINES ~